Better Guitar Wi......

Rockschool

A *Rockschool* Publication
245 Sandycombe Road, Kew, Richmond, Surrey, TW9 3EW

S.1480

1399

Welcome To *Guitar* Grade 1

Welcome to the Rockschool *Guitar* Grade 1 pack. The book and CD contain everything needed to play guitar in this grade. In the book you will find the exam scores in both standard notation and TAB. The CD has full stereo mixes of each tune, backing tracks to play along with for practice and tuning notes. Handy tips on playing the pieces and the marking schemes can be found in the Guru's Guide on page 15. If you have any queries about this or any other Rockschool exam, please call us on **020 8332 6303** or email us at office@rockschool.co.uk or visit our website http://www.rockschool.co.uk. Good luck!

Entry Zone Techniques in Debut and Grade 1

The eight Rockschool grades are divided into four Zones. Grade 1 *Guitar*, along with Debut, is part of the *Entry Zone*. This Zone is for players who are just starting out and who are looking to build a solid technical and stylistic foundation for their playing.

Debut: in Debut *Guitar* you will be concentrating on playing tunes. A player of Debut standard should be able to play up to 16 bars of music in 4/4 time, using simple first position melodies composed of whole, half and quarter notes and associated rests, as well as a range of basic first position chords. The pieces very often use open strings and melodies move between adjacent strings only.

Grade 1: in this grade you are asked to play three performance pieces, one of which may be a non-Rockschool piece. A player of grade 1 standard should be able to play up to 20 bars of music using first position chords and melodies composed of whole, half, quarter and eighth notes, dotted quarter notes and rests. Performances should include basic legato and vibrato playing.

The *Guitar* Grade 1 Exam

Players wishing to enter for a *Guitar* Grade 1 exam need to prepare **three** pieces, of which **one** may be a free choice piece chosen from outside the printed repertoire. In addition, you must prepare the technical excercises in this book, undertake either a sight reading test or an improvisation & interpretation test, take an ear test and answer general musicianship questions. Samples of these are printed in this book.

You can find more information on the *Guitar* Grade 1 exam in the Guru's Guide on page 15.

Guitar Tablature Explained
Guitar music in this book is notated in both standard notation and tablature

THE MUSICAL STAVE shows pitches and rhythms and is divided by lines into bars. Pitches are named after the first seven letters of the alphabet.

TABLATURE graphically represents the guitar fingerboard. Each horizontal line represents a string, and each number represents a fret.

Notes:

Strings:

4th string, 2nd fret — 1st & 2nd strings open, played together — open D chord

Definitions For Special Guitar Notation

HAMMER ON: Pick the lower note, then sound the higher note by fretting it without picking.

PULL OFF: Pick the higher note then sound the lower note by lifting the finger without picking.

SLIDE: Pick the first note, then slide to the next with the same finger.

STRING BENDS: Pick the first note then bend (or release the bend) to the pitch indicated in brackets.

GLISSANDO: Pick the note and slide along the string in the direction indicated.

VIBRATO: Vibrate the note by bending and releasing the string smoothly and continuously.

TRILL: Rapidly alternate between the two bracketed notes by hammering on and pulling off.

NATURAL HARMONICS: Lightly touch the string above the indicated fret then pick to sound a harmonic.

PINCHED HARMONICS: Bring the thumb of the picking hand into contact with the string immediately after the pick.

PICK HAND TAP: Strike the indicated note with a finger from the picking hand. Usually followed by a pull off.

FRET HAND TAP: As pick hand tap, but use fretting hand. Usually followed by a pull off or hammer on.

QUARTER TONE BEND: Pick the note indicated and bend the string up by a quarter tone.

- (accent) • Accentuate note (play it louder).
- (accent) • Accentuate note with great intensity.
- (staccato) • Shorten time value of note.
- • Downstroke
- • Upstroke

D.%. al Coda

D.C. al Fine

tacet

- Go back to the sign (%), then play until the bar marked *To Coda* ⊕ then skip to the section marked ⊕ *Coda*.
- Go back to the beginning of the song and play until the bar marked *Fine* (end).
- Instrument is silent (drops out).
- Repeat bars between signs.
- When a repeated section has different endings, play the first ending only the first time and the second ending only the second time.

Leaner

John Eacott

Gene Smith

Matt Backer

Who Knows

Hussein Boon

Midnite Movie

Deirdre Cartwright

Hard Case

Deirdre Cartwright

♩=100 *70's Rock*

Shaken Not Stirred

Deirdre Cartwright

Technical Exercises

In this section, the examiner will ask you to play a selection of exercises drawn from each of the two groups shown below. These exercises contain examples of the kinds of scales and arpeggios you can use when playing the pieces. You do not need to memorise the exercises (and can use the book in the exam) but the examiner will be looking for the speed of your response. The examiner will also give credit for the level of your musicality.

The exercises should be prepared in the keys and octaves specified. The TAB fingerings shown below are suggestions only. The exercises should be played at ♩ = 70. The examiner will give you this tempo in the exam.

Group A: Scales

Major scales

C major

Minor scales

A minor

Pentatonic scales

G major pentatonic

E minor pentatonic

Group B: Arpeggios

E major (lower octave)

E minor (lower octave)

Sight Reading *or* Improvisation & Interpretation

In this section you have a choice between either a sight reading test or an improvisation & interpretation test. Printed below is an example of the type of **sight reading** test you are likely to encounter in the exam. The piece will be composed in one of the four following styles: blues, rock, funk or jazz. The examiner will allow you 90 seconds to prepare it and will set the tempo for you on a metronome.

Printed below is an example of the type of **improvisation & interpretation** test you are likely to encounter in an exam. You will be asked to play an improvised line over a set of chord changes lasting 4 bars in one of the following styles: blues, rock, funk or jazz. The examiner will allow you 90 seconds to prepare it and will set the tempo for you on a metronome.

Ear Tests

You will find two ear tests in this grade. The examiner will play each test to you twice on CD. You will find two examples of the type of test you will get in the exam printed below.

Test 1

You will be asked to play back on your guitar a simple melody consisting of the first three notes of the G major scale (Root open G, A & B), adjacent scale tones, quarter notes only. 2 bars. You will be given the tonic note and will hear the sequence twice.

Test 2

You will also be asked to clap back the rhythm of a simple two bar melody after hearing it twice.

General Musicianship Questions

You will be asked five General Musicianship Questions at the end of the exam.

Topics:

i) Music theory
ii) Knowledge of your instrument

The music theory questions will cover the following topics at this grade:

> Recognition of pitches
> Note values
> Rests
> Time signatures
> Key signatures

Knowledge of the construction of the following chord types:

> Major
> Minor

Questions on these topics will be drawn from one of the pieces that you have played in the exam.

The instrument knowledge questions will cover the following topics at this grade:

> Plugging into the amplifier and the guitar
> Volume and tone adjustments on the guitar

Knowledge of parts of the guitar:

> Fretboard, neck, body, tuning pegs, nut, pickups,
> bridge, pickup selectors, scratchplate, and jack socket

The Guru's Guide to *Guitar* Grade 1

This section contains some handy hints compiled by Rockschool's Guitar Guru to help you get the most out of the performance pieces. Remember, these tunes are your chance to show your musical imagination and personality.

The TAB fingerings are suggestions only. Feel free to use different neck positions as they suit you. Please also note the solos featured in the full mixes are not meant to be indicative of the standard required for the grade.

Guitar Grade 1 Tunes

Rockschool tunes help you play the hit tunes you enjoy. The pieces have been written by top pop and rock composers and players according to style specifications drawn up by Rockschool.

The tunes printed here are divided into two groups of three pieces. The first group of pieces belongs to the *contemporary mainstream* and features current styles in today's charts. The second group of pieces consists of *roots styles*, those classic grooves and genres which influence every generation of performers.

CD full mix track 1, backing track 8: *Leaner*

A powerful drum 'n' bass track using bold sustained open position chords followed by some very simple melodic lines. Make sure that the strings are struck properly when playing the chords to achieve maximum effect. The remainder is very straightforward.

Composer: John Eacott. John is a prolific television and film composer and he has played with a wide range of artists including Goldie.

CD full mix track 2, backing track 9: *Gene Smith*

A noisy BritPop tune in the style of Oasis. This features strong chord patterns with most of the action in the picking hand. Make sure you grip the pick and hit the strings firmly using either up-down motions or downstrokes as required. There is a simple melody between the two sets of chords.

Composer: Matt Backer. Matt has a diverse list of playing credits that includes Joe Cocker, Steve Earle, Sinead O'Connor, Michael Ball and Steve Coogan's Latin superstar Tony Ferrino.

CD full mix track 3, backing tack 10: *Who Knows*

This is a hip R&B track inspired by Erikah Badou. This simple melody-line picks out the shapes suggested by the underlying chords. Note how the minor of Dm7 and Dm9 is resolved to the major under the Amaj7.

Composer: Hussein Boon. A purveyor of 'noisy pop' and drum 'n' bass, Hussein has played with the likes of Microgroove, Beats International, Omar and Karen Ramirez.

CD full mix track 4, backing track 11: *Midnite Movie*

A Blues Brothers-type soul track featuring simple stabbed chords (note the dots, or staccato markings under the notes) for the most part and a melodic line using quarter and eighth notes between the main chord sections. Accuracy and attack are important here as is an overdriven sound, so don't be shy.

Composer: Deirdre Cartwright. Deirdre fronted the TV *Rockschool* series in the 1980's and now plays and teaches guitar extensively across Europe.

CD full mix track 5, backing track 12: *Hard Case*

A rock track built around a simple opening riff which also incorporates a passing note, in this case G♯. The chords are bold and sustained so make sure you hold them on for their full values and the Am is strummed in eighth notes, before returning to the riff to finish.

Composer: Deirdre Cartwright.

CD full mix track 6, backing track 13: *Shaken not Sturred*

A mid tempo rock and roll track with overtones of Peter Green. The first half of this piece is a chord workout using simple variations of D and A. The melody is written in the pentatonic or five note scale, which is one of the most common guitar scales used in popular music along with the blues scale.

Composer: Deirdre Cartwright.

CD Musicians:

> **Guitars:** Simon Eyre   **Bass:** Geoff Gascoyne   **Drums:** Steve Creese
> **Keyboards and programming:** Adrian York

Grade Exam Marking Scheme

The table below shows the marking scheme for the *Guitar* Grade 1 exam.

ELEMENT	PASS	MERIT	DISTINCTION
Piece 1 Piece 2 Piece 3	13 out of 20 13 out of 20 13 out of 20	15 out of 20 15 out of 20 15 out of 20	17+ out of 20 17+ out of 20 17+ out of 20
Technical Exercises	11 out of 15	12 out of 15	13+ out of 15
Either: Sight Reading *Or:* Improvisation & Interpretation	6 out of 10	7 out of 10	8+ out of 10
Ear Tests	6 out of 10	7 out of 10	8+ out of 10
General Musicianship Questions	3 out of 5	4 out of 5	5 out of 5
Total Marks	**Pass: 65% +**	**Pass: 75% +**	**Pass: 85% +**

Free Choice Song Criteria

You can bring in your own performance pieces to play in the *Guitar* Grade 1 Exam. In this exam you can bring in **one** piece.

To help you choose your free choice piece, you should read the following criteria carefully.

- Players may bring in either their own compositions or songs already in the public domain, including hits from the charts.

- Songs may be performed either solo or to a CD backing track.

- Players should bring in two copies of the piece to be performed, notated either in standard notation, chord charts or TAB. Players must use an original copy of the tune to be performed, and must provide a second copy for the examiner, which may be a photocopy. For copyright reasons, photocopies handed to the examiner will be retained and destroyed by Rock School in due course.

- Players may perform either complete songs or extracts such as a solo part.

- Players should aim to keep their free choice song below 2 minutes in length.

- Players should aim to make each free choice song of a technical standard similar to those published in the Rockschool *Guitar* Grade 1 book. However, examiners will be awarding credit for how well you perform the song. In general, you should aim to play songs that mix the following physical and expressive techniques and rhythm skills.

Physical Techniques: players should be able to use a pick or the first two fingers of the picking hand, basic damping techniques to create rests, and the ability to move smoothly between chords and single notes.

Expressive Techniques: players should be able to display basic legato and staccato techniques.

Rhythm skills: players should use pieces which use a mixture of whole, half, quarter and eighth notes as well as dotted quarter notes. Some simple syncopations are allowed.

You, or your teacher, may wish to adapt an existing piece of music to suit the criteria above. You should ensure that any changes to the music are clearly marked on the sheet submitted to the examiner.

Entering Rockschool Exams

Entering a Rockschool exam is easy. Please read through these instructions carefully before filling in the exam entry form. Information on current exam fees can be obtained from Rock School by ringing **020 8332 6303**

- You should enter for a *Guitar* Grade 1 exam when you feel ready.

- You can enter for any one of three examination periods. These are shown below with their closing dates.

PERIOD	DURATION	CLOSING DATE
Period A	1st February to 15th March	1st December
Period B	15th May to 31st July	1st April
Period C	1st November to 15th December	1st October

These dates will apply from 1st January 1999 until further notice

- Please fill in the form giving your name, address and phone number. Please tick the type and level of exam, along with the period and year. Finally, fill in the fee box with the appropriate amount. You should send this form with a cheque or postal order to: **Rockschool, 245 Sandycombe Road, Kew, Richmond, Surrey, TW9 2EW**

- When you enter an exam you will receive from Rockschool an acknowledgement letter containing your exam entry number along with a copy of our exam regulations.

- Rockschool will allocate your entry to a centre and you will receive notification of the exam, showing a date, location and time as well as advice of what to bring to the centre.

- You should inform Rockschool of any cancellations or alterations to the schedule as soon as you can as it is usually not possible to transfer entries from one centre, or one period, to another without the payment of an additional fee.

- Please bring your music book and CD to the exam. You may not use photocopied music, nor the music used by someone else in another exam. The examiner will stamp each book after each session. You may be barred from taking an exam if you use someone else's music.

- You should aim to arrive for your *Guitar* Grade 1 exam fifteen minutes before the time stated on the schedule.

- The exam centre will have a waiting area and warm-up facilities which you may use prior to being called into the main exam room.

- Each *Guitar* Grade 1 exam is scheduled to last for 20 minutes. You can use a small proportion of this time to tune up and get ready.

- About 2 to 3 weeks after the exam you will receive a typed copy of the examiner's mark sheet. Every successful player will receive a Rockschool certificate of achievement.

Printed and bound in Great Britain by Caligraving Limited